BEHIND ENEMY LINES

A Field Manual For God's Army

Chuck Dean

BEHIND ENEMY LINES
Copyright © 1997 by Chuck Dean

Published by WinePress Publishing
PO Box 1406
Mukilteo, WA 98275

Except where noted, all Scripture verses are from the New
American Standard version of the Bible. Copyright © 1976,
1978 by The Moody Bible Institute of Chicago.

ISBN 1-57921-027-9
Library of Congress Number: 97-60775

FOR

DAVE, ROSS, KING
and all the others who have given their lives to
America's military services; and who have chosen to
give the remainder of their lives serving God on
His many fronts.

TABLE OF CONTENTS

PREFACE

FIGHT THE GOOD FIGHT!

We live in a world at war. If it isn't "hot war" it is "cold war." There is mounting tension between different nations, races and ideologies. Our homes are no refuge, for, even there, so often there is strife between husband and wife, between parents and children. People search in vain for a way out. An army drill instructor once said to a trainee, "Your platoon is almost surrounded, and you are running out of ammunition. As platoon commander, what steps would you take?"

"Long ones, sergeant," the new soldier replied.

Man has been surrounded since the fall of Adam and Eve, but he can't take long steps to escape his dilemma. He is like a hunted animal with nowhere to hide.

Humans are at war with humans because humans are at war with God. Behind the human battle there is a spiritual battle. It is the age-old fight between darkness and light, between good and evil, between God's children and Satan. Neutrality is virtually impossible. Each human is on one side or the other; not one of us can remain in a "no man's land" and claim to be unaffected by the war around us.

The Christian life means warfare. The battlefield, the weapons and the foe are all spiritual rather than material. When you decide to answer the call to Christ's service, you will soon find that you cannot ignore the war, and you will be asked to go "behind enemy lines" to conduct operations for the Lord. This book is designed to help you develop the required soldierly qualities needed to endure every "good fight." It is your field manual to victory in Jesus.

Assault the ambush!
Chuck Dean

CHAPTER ONE

PRE-MISSION BRIEFING

"Faith is not faith unless it contains an element of risk."
Elizabeth Elliot

MISSION OBJECTIVE:
THE PURPOSE OF A FIELD MANUAL

There are two kinds of Christian soldiers: one who serves in the army and one who goes to war. What do I mean? One soldier actively engages the enemy, using God-given authority, and hones his combat skills for daily victories. The other has false notions that there is no war going on at all. He flirts with the world and accepts its lies. He doubts and has unbelief about spiritual enemies and may even harbor the view that Satan is a doctrinal myth. This kind of Christian is a serious liability to God's plan in wrestling the "prisoners of war" from the chains of the devil. Sadly enough, a large portion of the church now falls into this category. So, who needs this manual? Every Christian…but only some will find it's true value and use it.

Behind Enemy Lines is meant for ministers and missionaries because their work is so vital (the Great Commission, Matthew 28:19–20). Schooled and trained to be salt and light to a dying world, they have been sent as emissaries of the church for hundreds of years. However, many are sent to their assignments ill-equipped to stand against the schemes of Satan. They soon become ineffective, casualties of war because they didn't know about, or refused to heed, the biblical warnings regarding spiritual warfare.

Seminary professors charged with training missionaries may refuse to teach about Satan, too. They might skip over the Bible sections dealing with him, and never take the time to point out that the Apostle Paul was serious when he wrote Ephesians, chapter 6. Consequently hundreds of missionaries face each day confused and defeated. As a result, they ignore the primary work of the Lord, which is saving souls (Acts 26:18).

From this cause, new soldiers (missionaries, etc.) arrive at their "duty stations" unaware of the wiles of the devil. At the first hint of an enemy assault on their position, they shrink back and compromise. They may justify it by serving strictly in "humanitarian" endeavors instead. Why? Because they don't understand or believe that their opposition is spiritual. When this happens, Satan is given liberty to prowl about freely in their lives and the lives of those they are sent to deliver from the darkness of eternal death. They never get to the job they were sent to do.

In my times of going to the mission field, the schemes of the devil have been at work against me. Sometimes I have readily recognized them and sometimes not. I also know this is true of every missionary sent by God to do His work, whether they want to admit it or not. Those who believe that God's Word is for today and expect enemy opposition will do better than those who don't. The ones who study the Scriptures and allow the Holy Spirit to train them in warfare strategies will do the best. It is the intent of this book to assist in that training.

"MISSION FIELD" DEFINED

I like my church. The congregation (especially the pastors) consider every service to be the mission field. In fact, over the doors as you leave, a large sign reads: "You are now entering the mission field." We are always reminded of our position in the Body and what we are called to do every time we leave the building.

You see, my church believes that everyone is called—no matter who we are or what we do. And everywhere we go there is missionary work waiting. I don't know about others, but I find a degree of comfort in having an assignment each time I walk out into the world. Perhaps this church could be a model for others to follow.

COMBAT OPERATION

During my years of military service and continued interest in such things, I have easily been able to relate human warfare to its spiritual counterpart. It is my way of keeping it all straight. In this respect, maybe I can help you better understand God's intentions and designs for warfare, too.

With that said, let's look at a basic military procedure—planning out a combat operation. A lot is done prior to any combat operation. Being prepared with good intelligence is mandatory. After all, nobody likes to get caught fumbling around in the dark...especially when lives are at stake.

One crucial pre-planning topic is the nature of the terrain or ground you will be fighting on. You must have a clear understanding and knowledge of the terrain, or you are well-advised not to attempt any tactical operations on it. It is the same in Christian missionary deployment. Know what ground, and *whose* ground, you are operating on before setting out.

I simply look at the mission field as an area where a combat operation is being conducted. A missionary steps out and begins to minister God's truths to the unsaved. When he does, it is like being dropped behind enemy lines—he enters Satan's territory, and nearly always smack-dab in the middle of his camp.

So, exactly what is the Christian mission field? It is terrain, not *our* terrain, but Satan's. Every time we go out to do the Lord's work we are on the enemy's turf. Most likely you will find this "terrain" right in the hearts of the men and women you run into.

Which brings us to the next point: The mission field is not so much where you go, but what you do. Just like evangelism is not a formula; it is a life lived and given to others, no matter where you are.

The mission field isn't necessarily a place, like a jungle full of half-naked natives. It may not be a starving, communist-ravaged, third world country either. The mission field is many places and many people. It is our neighborhoods, places of work, schools, social clubs, and even our churches. It may be your teenager's best friend that comes to visit. And, yes, it could be the Hottentot people in a land far away. The mission field is *people*: people far and near, next door, or the uttermost parts of the earth.

So, why is it that we tend to think that praying with naked heathens in a steaming jungle is the "work" of a missionary, and praying with the three-piece-suit heathens on Madison Avenue isn't? It's a mindset, and a mindset is a powerful, clandestine weapon of the devil. It is used against us to prevent widespread evangelism and discipleship. We need to know this to be combat-ready soldiers for God.

A combat operation is the action you take in your mission field. Let it be done to the glory of the Lord.

CHAPTER TWO

"CHAPTER VI"—
A MISSIONARY'S STORY

"Truth not experienced is no better than absolute error."
A. W. Tozer

A SEARCH FOR TRUTH

As with many vital tools the Lord has used to instruct His warriors over the centuries, the following excerpt surfaces from an existence of relative obscurity. I have found it to be a powerful weapon in the hands of Christian soldiers.

A few years ago a missionary friend passed along "Chapter VI" of a book that was never completed or published. He picked it up on one of his many journeys for the Lord. My friend was not acquainted with the author, Mr. Wilbur Pickering.

"Chapter VI" is one of those rare works that crosses denominational barriers in teaching on a topic that has been shrouded with controversy. Mr. Pickering speaks with a knowledge akin to Josh McDowell and the common sense of Dean Sherman in regards to spiritual warfare. Pickering's accounts are from first-hand experience on the mission field, and there is little doubt that this writing has God's fingerprints on it. "Chapter VI" will stretch your Christian walk. After reading it, you will be convinced, like I was, that it was written by a battle-tested man who obviously was commissioned by God to share it with us.

Wilbur Pickering was a missionary to Brazil, and after failing on his first missionary assignment, he came home to begin a search for truth in the matter of spiritual warfare. What he writes here is vital information that every Christian warrior must have in order to be prepared for the work of the Great Commission.

He writes:

Now let's consider the words of the Lord Jesus that we find in Acts 26:18. Paul is recounting, years afterward, the encounter he had with Him on the road to Damascus. Here's his story:

"13 At midday, O king, along the road I saw a light from heaven, brighter than the sun, shining around me and those who journeyed with me.

14 And when we all had fallen to the ground, I heard a voice speaking to me and saying in the Hebrew language, "Saul, Saul, why are you persecuting me? It is hard for you to kick against the goads."

16

15 So I said, "Who are you, Lord?" And he said, "I am Jesus, whom you are persecuting.

16 But rise and stand on your feet; for I have appeared to you for this purpose, to make you a minister and a witness both of the things which you have seen and of the things which I will yet reveal to you.

17 I will deliver you from the people, as well as from the Gentiles to whom I now send you,

18 to open their eyes and to bring them back, from darkness to light and from the power of Satan to God, so that they may receive forgiveness of sins and an inheritance among those who are sanctified by faith in me."

Of specific interest to us here is the missionary commission that Paul (he was called Saul then) received…Matthew 28:19, Mark 16:15 and Acts 1:8 took place between the resurrection and the ascension, but to commission Paul, Jesus returned from Heaven! One other detail deserves special notice—the responsibility that Paul received was primarily for the nations, ("Gentiles" is a translation of the same word that in Mt. 28:19 is rendered "nations"). For these reasons it seems that this missionary commission takes on a special importance for us. And all the more so for whoever is going to do transcultural work. So let's consider this commission in more detail.

PAUL'S MISSIONARY COMMISSION

Paul is sent to the nations, (defined ethnically) "...*to open their eyes and bring them back, from darkness to light and from the power of Satan to God, so that they may receive forgiveness of sins and a place among those who are sanctified by faith in Me.*" In other words, before someone can receive forgiveness of sins, even that someone must be freed from the power of Satan! Were you aware of that? Well, there it is. Before a person can be saved, someone must do something about Satan's influence upon him.

The Lord Jesus had already said the same thing in different words during His earthly ministry. We find it in Mark 3:27. "*No man can plunder the strong man's goods, invading his house, unless he first bind the strong man; then he may plunder his house.*" I have used the definite article with the first occurrence of "*strong man*" because the Greek text has it, the point being that this particular strong man has already been introduced in the immediate context. "*The strong man*" here is Satan. (The Jewish leaders tried to explain Jesus' authority over the demons by saying that He expelled them by the power of Beelzebub, prince of the demons. In His retort Jesus doesn't waste time with that name but uses the enemy's proper name, Satan.)

So then, the Lord Jesus declares that it is impossible to steal Satan's goods unless you bind him first. And what might the nature of those "goods" be? In the context (of the above Scripture) Jesus had (just) delivered someone from a demon that caused blindness and dumbness. In their comments the scribes and Pharisees include other

18

instances where Jesus had expelled demons. It seems clear that the *"goods"* are people who are subject to Satan's power, in one way or another. Thus we have the same essential truth as that declared in Acts 26:18—we have to do something about Satan's power over a person so that he or she can be saved! But what does Satan do to people that makes it necessary to *"bind"* him?

We find the answer in 2 Corinthians 4:4. Let's begin with verse 3. *"If our gospel is veiled it is veiled to them who are perishing, in whom the god of this age has blinded the minds of the unbelievers so that the light of the gospel of the glory of Christ, who is the image of God, should not shine in them."* The Text clearly states that Satan, "the god of this world," is in the business of blinding the minds of unbelievers when they hear the Gospel, so they won't understand, so they won't be convicted, so they won't repent and convert.

This is a terrible truth, the most terrible truth in the world, at least as I see it. The enemy has access to our minds, access in the sense that he has the power/ability to invade them, whether by introducing thoughts or by jamming our reasoning. The Lord Jesus had already declared this truth previously, when He explained the parable of the sower. *"These are the ones by the wayside where the word is sown; but, as soon as they hear it Satan comes and takes away the word that was planted in their hearts"* (Mk. 4:15). In the parallel passage in Luke 8:12 Jesus adds the following words: *"lest they believe and be saved."* Note that the Word is already in the mind or heart of the person, but then Satan comes, invades the mind and "takes away" that Word. I'm not sure just how this intrusion by the enemy works, perhaps he causes a mental block of some sort, but the practical effect is that the Word becomes ineffective, as if the person hadn't even heard it.

THE STRATEGIC EFFECT

It seems obvious to me that whoever doesn't take this truth into account will be condemning himself to produce little effect in the spiritual realm, to work hard and achieve little. And isn't that exactly what we see? We preach, we evangelize, we speak and do so much, and yet the results are usually sparse, especially the lasting ones. So much so that we easily become discouraged and think of quitting. Isn't that so? But my brother, before preaching or talking did you give yourself the trouble to forbid the enemy's interference in the thoughts of your hearer? If not, what do you expect? It was Jesus Himself, God the Son here in this world, who made it clear that we must bind Satan in order to be able to remove people from his "house." We must bind Satan so as to avoid his interference in the minds of those who are being evangelized. (I will explain how to bind Satan later when I discuss the weapons that are at our disposal.) Now then, this "coin" has two sides: our efficiency and our success depend upon our binding the enemy; but if we don't bind him we become his accomplices, because by permitting his interference without doing anything about it we cooperate with him! Can you imagine that? Actually, I suspect that few have in fact "imagined" since these truths receive little or no mention in our churches, institutes and seminaries, at least so far. But really, brethren, the time has come, don't you think?

I went to the Amazon jungle in 1963 in order to begin our ministry among the Apuring people (along the Purus river in the state of Amazonas, Brazil). So far as I know I was the first one to challenge Satan's dominion over this people, a total domination down through the centuries. My basic purpose in being there was to see if I could remove that people from Satan's house and take them to Jesus' house, if I could transfer them from the kingdom of darkness to the kingdom of light. But unfortunately, in spite of a Master of Theology degree and having read the Bible through several times, I was not aware of these truths. I got clobbered!

I got it without mercy, until I had had enough. Satan wiped the floor with me. He didn't think my idea was the least bit funny, and I didn't know how to defend myself. Actually, I didn't really understand what was happening. You see, I was skeptical about the activity of the demons. Oh yes, I knew that Satan and the demons exist, because the Bible is clear and emphatic on that score, but I knew very little about how they operate and virtually nothing about the use of our weapons, whether for defense or offense. My theological background, both formal and informal, was strictly "traditional"—casting out demons and things of that sort was "Pentecostal." My professors transmitted the idea that a servant of Christ was untouchable or exempt from demonic attack; that sort of thing wouldn't be a problem for us.

Anyhow, I got clobbered. First, my wife and I were attacked in the mind, (and then) in the body. Second, being skeptical on the subject I wasn't able to hide my skepticism. (These) people have to deal with demons. This relationship is central to their culture. Since they know that the demons both exist and attack them in various ways, as in fact they do indeed exist and attack, my skepticism disqualified me. I was there proposing to teach them about spiritual truth, about supernatural things, but was obviously ignorant about the central reality of their existence. I lost my credibility. Third, in consequence (of my skepticism and ignorance) I was unable to help or liberate them. I was unable to give them proof of Christ's power, and therefore of the value of the Gospel…. Fourth, when you finally control the language and culture to the point where you can explain about Jesus—what He's like, what He did, what He taught—then, sooner or later, you will say that He expelled demons and cured the effects of their activity. At last you said something that the people really want to know. (As I've already explained, they "worship" the demons out of necessity, not because they enjoy it, because they don't know of any benevolent power great enough to free them.) Now you have their attention and can expect this query: *Jesus has power over the demons?!*

At this point you have a choice: are you going to say that Jesus has power, or that He had it? What are you going to affirm? I imagine that you would say, "Yes, He

22

has!" Right? Only at that point a demon will challenge you to your face, attacking someone in the village. So now what do you do? You don't know how to cast out demons, you are skeptical about such things, and yet you affirm that Jesus has power over them. If you don't know how to impose the victory and power of Christ in that hour, if you can't prove that Jesus is greater, then you were just beating your gums. You will be demoralized. You lied! Worse yet, Jesus is demoralized too! Of course— you are His only spokesman in that place and if you can't demonstrate His power, the people will certainly conclude that He doesn't have such power. Any doubt about that? Well, I got clobbered. I weep when I think on the little that I achieved among the Apuring people, on behalf of Christ's kingdom, compared with what I could and should have achieved, had I understood this missionary strategy of Christ: free the peoples from the power of Satan.

And that's not all. The great majority of the missionaries actually working (and that have already worked) among the animistic peoples of the world are skeptical about these things, like I was. Sadly, our missionary organizations have not concerned themselves about this matter, as a rule. The missionaries are out there suffering, as I did, producing much less effect than they could produce. What a tragedy! What a waste, in every sense of the term! The strategic importance of this matter is tremendous. If one day we reach the point of sending out workers who are adequately prepared in this area and of having churches full of people who know how to conduct spiritual warfare, then we will finish reaching the world. (Even the Islamic world, which I believe to be the most difficult challenge that we face, should be reachable in this way, because they too are troubled by demons.)

We have yet to comment upon the last phrase of Paul's commission, *"a place among those who are sanctified."* I would say that the primary reference of this phrase is to final sanctification, our position in Christ. It happens, however, that it could easily refer to our experience as well because what Satan and the demons do has a definite influence on our spiritual life and on the effectiveness of our ministry, as well as on our life in general.

My, how the enemy messes up our lives, spoils our homes, dilutes our efficiency in the work! If we would convince ourselves about the extent of their activity and learn how to handle the spiritual weapons that Christ gives us we could simply transform our lives, our homes and our ministries. The majority of the people that God calls to transcultural mission are defeated by Satan right here— they never get to the field. Of the few, relatively speaking, that do get to the mission field, half are removed from the running within four years—they return defeated to their home countries, and never again return to the mission field. Such have been the statistics of modern missions, but I sincerely believe that we can improve the picture dramatically. All we have to do is get serious about this missionary strategy of Christ: *liberate people from the power of Satan.* It is absolutely necessary that we recognize that we are at war.

The Spiritual War

We are in a war whose sphere is universal and which provides the context from which everything we do derives its deepest importance. In Luke 11:23 the Lord Jesus said: "Whoever is not for me is against me; and whoever does not gather with me scatters." Jesus does not allow neutrality—you are either for or against, one or the other. Either we are gathering or else we are scattering and therefore there is no neutral ground. We may grant that a given object is presumably neutral in itself, but the use that we make of it will not be neutral. At the deepest level we either do things with a view to God's kingdom and glory or we do them for some other reason, and be that reason what it may it will serve the interests of the enemy. "Whoever does not gather with me, scatters." It follows that everything we do is invested with importance. Even the ordinary things that we usually do without thinking have consequences in the spiritual realm. We are at war, whether we know it or not and whether we like it or not.

We can state the problem more precisely. Not only are we at war, we are on the front line. That is to say, there is lead flying around on all sides. To walk around on a field of battle without taking due precaution is simply stupid, too stupid; it is to guarantee that you will be hit. The more so when we are precisely the ones who are in the enemy's sights because we belong to Jesus.

One of the principle passages on the spiritual war is Ephesians 6:10–19 (the full armor of God). It says plainly that our fight is not against people ("flesh and blood"), but against evil spirit beings who are organized in a hierarchy, a veritable army. It speaks of "the wiles of the devil"; it speaks of "the fiery darts of the wicked one." It is urgent that we know the enemy, but first I want to mention another factor.

THE GUARANTEE OF THE STRATEGY

In Hebrews 2:14 we find the truth that renders this strategy viable. *"Since, then, the children partake of flesh and blood, he also himself likewise shared in the same things so that through his death he might destroy the one who had the power of death, that is, the devil."* Why did Jesus die? To destroy Satan! Did you know that? Well it's true, and He succeeded! Hallelujah! Colossians 2:15, Ephesians 1:20–22 and John 16:11 speak of the defeat suffered by Satan and his angels, the demons. That's why we read that he "had" the power of death (Hebrews was written after Christ's victory). In Revelation 1:18 the glorified Jesus declares: "I have the keys of death and hades." Jesus won! It is Christ's victory that guarantees this strategy and makes it viable. We can, yes we can, liberate people from the power of Satan!

How do Satan and the Demons Operate?

Let's go directly to the Sacred Text. We'll begin with Luke 9:18–22:

18 It came to pass that as he was alone praying his disciples came to him, and he asked them, saying, "Who do the multitudes say that I am?"

19 Answering they said, "John the baptist; others say, Elijah; still others say that one of the ancient prophets has resurrected."

20 He said to them, "But you, who do you say that I am?" Peter answered and said, "The Christ of God."

21 Warning them he ordered them not to tell anyone, saying,

22 "It is necessary that the Son of man should suffer many things, that he be rejected by the elders, the chief priests and the scribes, that he be killed and that he rise from the dead on the third day."

I wish to call attention to the grammatical structure of this passage. Note the present participles: "answering", "warning" and "saying." The effect of this structure is to signal continuous action. Verses 18–22 contain a single conversation. Having registered this fact let's move to the parallel passage in Matthew 16:13–23 which gives us some more detail. Rather than transcribe the whole thing I will just comment on the added details. In verse 16 Peter answers, "You are the Christ, Son of the Living God," to which He responds, "You are blessed, Simon, son of Jonah, because it was not flesh and blood that revealed this to you but *my Father who is in Heaven"* (vs. 17). Skipping to verse 21 we have Jesus' declaration that He must suffer and die. With that Peter began to rebuke Him: *"Far be it from you, Lord; this shall never happen to you!"* (vs. 22). To which initiative Jesus answered, *"Get behind me, Satan!"* (vs. 23).

Well, that scares me; that sends shivers up my spine. Within three minutes, or five at the most (we saw in Luke that this was a single conversation), Peter spoke two times. The first time it was God who put the words in Peter's mouth. It was Jesus Christ, God the Son on earth, who explained the true nature of the transaction. Peter did not speak on his own but moved by the Father. So far so good; that God can do something like that comes as no surprise. It is the second time that is bothersome because this time it was Satan who put the words in Peter's mouth! Again, it is Jesus Christ, God the Son on earth, who explains the true nature of the transaction. When He uses the enemy's proper name, Satan, His meaning is inescapable. It really was Satan.

The rules of language do not permit the "spiritualizing" of someone's proper name (unless it be in a secret code, which deliberately violates those rules—but that is not the case here). "Gerald" always refers to someone of that name, and so with "Samuel," or "Charles," etc. "Satan" here refers precisely to Satan. Once again we are face to face with the most terrible truth that there is in this

life, at least as I see it. *The enemy has access to our minds,
he can put words in our mouths.* I wish in the worst way
that it wasn't true, but my wishes don't change reality.

THEY ATTACK OUR MINDS

When I finally awakened to this truth I began to understand several things that used to happen to me. More
than once I would be talking with someone, a serious
conversation about the things of God, when all of a sudden words would come from my mouth that were simply
unacceptable, words that destroyed the situation. As soon
as I had spoken I knew it was bad, but it was too late; the
other person would turn his back and leave. I was left
dismayed and perplexed. How could I say something
like that? Note well, it wasn't something I had been thinking about, that had been in my mind; no, I became aware
of it only after I had spoken. For years I never found an
answer, I couldn't figure out what happened to me, but
now I know. Some demon put those words in my mouth,
and since I didn't realize such a thing was possible I fell
into the trap. Now that no longer happens to me. Now I
know how to defend myself.

I know. You don't like this idea (neither do I), you
don't want to accept it. Let's go slowly. Maybe you yourself never experienced anything like I just described but
perhaps you have observed the following. It is routine,
you can virtually count on it; in any meeting where the

progress of the work is being handled (be it of the dea-cons, elders or trustees; of the board of a mission or a school; of a presbytery, synod or conference; in short, be it a small or large gathering) you can observe the follow-ing. Everything is going well, the blessed communion of the saints seems to be functioning, when all of a sudden someone says something he shouldn't, gratuitously, to no good purpose. The climate of the meeting is ruined; you may as well go home for all the constructive progress that will now be made.

Haven't you ever seen that happen? I bet you have; it is routine. You can even call that person aside, after the meeting, and ask: "Tell me, please, why did you ever say that?" And if he is sincere, as he often is, he may answer something like this: "To be perfectly frank with you, I don't know!" And it will be the truth, for he was simply an instrument in the hand of the enemy—a demon put those words in his mouth, and that was it!

AGAINST PRAYER

You still don't like it? You are still resisting the idea? Then let's think about prayer. Please tell me, when you set yourself to pray, to intercede, to really seek God's face (let's say when you plan to spend at least fifteen minutes), does everything go well? Are you able to concentrate your thoughts in prayer without problem? I bet not. Don't your thoughts wander? All of a sudden you think of a conver-sation you had, about an unfinished job, about something that happened six months ago—no? Let's analyze this together. Your thoughts were concentrated on God, right? You didn't have idle thoughts that were free to go looking for those things. So where did they come from? Isn't it obvious? It was demonic interference in your mind. Those extraneous thoughts don't have to be dirty or vile— if our thoughts are diverted away from prayer then the enemy has achieved his objective.

We need to understand something else about prayer. As soon as we start to pray we enter the spiritual sphere and with that the enemy gets busy. It is primarily in prayer that we wage spiritual war and the enemy feels a direct threat. So he goes into immediate action to distract us. You can put this down: no one remains alone when he prays—the moment you begin to pray in a serious way you will be "covered" or opposed by at least one demon (depending on how dangerous the enemy thinks you are).

This opposition may take various forms. If it isn't extraneous thoughts it is sleepiness. (When I was a boy we had a sure cure for insomnia. If I couldn't sleep my mother would say, "Just pray and you'll go right to sleep." Sure enough! I would start praying and in a few minutes I was snoring.) If it isn't sleepiness it's discouragement, or your mind goes blank or you feel fear. A homemaker finds a few moments and kneels to pray, and guess what happens. The telephone hasn't rung for a week but now it won't stop. She hasn't had any visitors for the longest time but at that exact moment the doorbell sounds. The children were playing quietly but all of a sudden a loud fight breaks out. If there are any dogs in the neighborhood they all start barking. Isn't that so? Remarkable, don't you think? We are at war, my brother!

AGAINST LIFE

The access that the enemy has to our minds can have drastic consequences. Consider the case of Ananias in Acts 5. Let's review the context. *"The multitude of those who believed were of one heart and of one soul; neither said any of them that any of the things which he possessed was his own; but they had all things common.... Neither was there any among them that lacked; for as many as were possessors of lands or houses sold them, and brought the prices of the things that were sold and laid them down at the apostles' feet; and distribution was made unto every man according as he had need"* (Acts 4:32–35). That was the situation that gave rise to the case of Ananias. Please stop here and read Acts 5:1–10.

As Peter explains, they didn't have to bring anything; or they could bring half, if they wished, as long as they didn't claim it was everything. Their problem was that they lied, wishing to receive credit as if they had brought the full amount. The apostle Peter affirms that it was Satan (again the proper name is used) who placed the idea in Ananias' mind, or heart. What was the result for Ananias? Death. Right? This is really heavy, people! A little later, in comes the wife: "Is that the way it was, Sapphira?"

"That's right." *Flop*—she died on the spot! This access that the enemy has to our minds can result in physical death! Recall that he "had the power of death" and by bluffing (or usurping) he continues to do virtually as he pleases. I suspect that we might go into shock if we knew how many people have died as a direct result of demonic activity. But that's not the worst of it. Consider the case of Judas...

In John 13:2 we read: "*Supper being ended, the devil having already put into the heart of Judas Iscariat, Simon's son, to betray him...*" While in John 13:27 we read: "*After supper Satan entered into him (Judas). Then Jesus said unto him, 'What you are going to do, do quickly.'*" (Cf. Luke 22:3.) The idea of betraying Jesus was put in Judas' heart by the devil. But at the crucial moment Satan, by name, "entered" into him, took control of him to guarantee that he would execute it. What was the result for Judas? Physical death, because a little later, overtaken by remorse (not repentance, which is different), he hanged himself. What further result did he receive? Spiritual death, because while praying to His own Father Jesus said, "*Those whom you gave me I have kept, and none of them is lost except the son of perdition, that the Scripture might be fulfilled*" (John 17:12). Note also Matthew 26:24: "*The Son of man goes as it is written of him; but woe unto that man by whom the Son of man is betrayed! It would have been good for that man if he had not been born.*" Judas was lost!

The enemy's interference in peoples minds not only can result in physical death, it can also result in spiritual death. Judas isn't the only one. If it were just Judas perhaps we could dismiss it—after all, Judas! Alas, no! We have already seen from 2 Corinthians 4:4 (also Mk. 4:15 and Lk. 8:12) that multitudes are going to hell as a result of Satan's interference in people's minds. (Since he is not omnipresent he works through a chain of command, using his angels, the demons.) This is a most serious matter—anything that results in the salvation of the soul, or the forfeiting of that salvation, is of maximum importance. To close our eyes to this matter is treason against our King.

OTHER EVIDENCES

I know, you still don't like it. Well, let's look at the Text some more. In 2 Corinthians 11:3 we are informed that "the serpent (Satan) corrupts our minds;" in the context it is the minds of believers. That's the interference in our thoughts. In James 3:2–12 we find a very interesting description with respect to our thesis:

02 *In many things we all stumble. If any man offend not in word the same is a perfect man, able also to bridle the whole body.*

03 *Behold, we put bits in the horses mouths so that they may obey us, and we turn about their whole body.*

04 *Behold also the ships; though they are so great and are*

driven by fierce winds, yet are they turned about with a very small helm, wherever the pilot wills.

05 Even so the tongue is a little member and boasts great things. Behold how great a matter a little fire kindles!

06 The tongue also is a fire, a world of iniquity; that is how the tongue is among our members, defiling the whole body and setting on fire the whole course of our existence, being itself set on fire by hell.

07 For every kind of beast and bird, of reptile and marine animal can be tamed and has been tamed by mankind;

08 but the tongue can no man tame, incorrigible evil that it is, full of deadly poison!

09 Therewith bless we God, even the Father, and therewith curse we men who are made in the likeness of God.

10 Out of the same mouth proceed blessing and cursing. My brethren, these things ought not so to be.

11 Does a spring send forth from the same opening both sweet water and bitter?

12 Can a fig tree, my brethren, yield olives, or a grapevine figs? Likewise no spring can give both salt water and fresh.

We know that in nature a spring never gives both sweet and bitter water, alternately; it isn't possible. But lets imagine that one day we came across such a spring: one minute the water was sweet, the next it was bitter, and so on. How could we explain such a thing? There would have to be two sources or veins feeding the spring, and they would have to meet just under the surface, taking turns. This is just what God's Word affirms happens with our mouths: first blessing and then cursing proceed from them. How can this be? In fact, the language in verses 2, 6 and 8 could strike us as peculiar—not to offend in word is to be perfect; the tongue contaminates the body and inflames the course of life; the tongue is a fire, a world of iniquity, an incorrigible evil, a deadly poison! How can we explain such language? Whatever is going on? I believe that the answer may be found at the end of verse 6.

What are we to understand when the Text says that the tongue "is set on fire by hell"? At the very least it must mean that the tongue receives its capacity or ability to inflame from "hell," and therefore owes its inflammatory activity to "hell." But who or what is "hell"? I believe this is an instance of metonymy (a figure of speech where a word is used in place of another which is intimately associated with it). With whom is hell most closely associated? With Satan, since it has been prepared precisely for him and his angels (Mt. 25:41). I take it that this passage attributes a large share of the damage that results from the wrong use of the tongue to the activity of Satan and the demons, influencing the thinking and speaking of human beings. To be sure, we can make wrong use of our tongues all by ourselves, no doubt about it, but the language of the Text demands a further explanation. There are two sources contributing to our speech, our own will and malignant interference. Be not deceived!

When you find yourself beside a stranger on a bus, train or plane, do you find it hard to converse with him? Say about the weather, fashions, politics or sports? Well, an introvert would presumably have difficulty, but most of us have little or no trouble. But if you shift the topic of conversation and start to talk about Jesus, then what happens? Do you speak as freely as you were? As a matter of fact, no. Correct? Don't you feel fear, get nervous, your mind goes blank, your palms get clammy? Why, do you suppose? Where does that fear come from? In 2 Timothy 1:7 we read: *"God has not given us a spirit of fear, but of power, of love and of self-control."* It goes on to say, *"Therefore do not be ashamed of testifying to our Lord."*

The spirit of fear that attacks us when we want to witness about Christ does not come from God. The Text is clear. So where does it come from? Whose interest does it serve if we don't talk about Christ? Isn't it obvious? When a believer finds it hard to talk about Jesus, instead of calling him a coward and loading him with guilt we should first rebuke the spirit of fear. Obviously we can be cowards without demonic assistance. Still, you may be sure that many times we are attacked by an evil spirit. Then there are those terrible nightmares. The person feels that he is being suffocated. (Actually, 400 years ago the word "nightmare" referred precisely to a demon that came and suffocated people while they slept.) If the demons can attack our minds while we are awake, how much more so while we are asleep and helpless (protection does exist—we must forbid any such interference before going to sleep; we can do this for others as well as for ourselves). Besides what happens in the mind, sometimes you can feel, or even see, an evil presence in the room. We are surrounded by the practice of spiritism of every sort (the criminal practices of satanists are getting more and more attention in the news media; more and more movies deal with the occult. Go to the library of your local high school and just see how many books on occult practices are available to the students).

The growing "New Age" movement has significant components of spiritism; and converted spiritists/satanists declare that they have infiltrated our churches, our schools, the whole society to an alarming extent. It becomes hard to understand how there can be disciples of Jesus who still don't believe in the existence of the demons, and in their activity, including an interference in our minds. I wouldn't be surprised if in a not too distant future almost the only people to remain skeptical about these things will be the members of certain Protestant churches. What a tragedy!

CHAPTER THREE

THE ACT OF WAR

"Spiritual warfare is not just a prayer prayed or a demon re-buked—it is a life lived."

Dean Sherman, YWAM

IDENTIFYING THE ENEMY

Before an army goes to war it must know who it is fighting. To know the enemy is to know its personality, its characteristics, its strengths, and its limitations. Only a foolish commander would launch operations against a force not knowing its assets and liabilities.

I was called into the ministry almost immediately after getting saved in 1986. The Lord sent me out to tell Vietnam veterans about His saving grace.

In the beginning I thought the enemy I was to fight against on their behalf was stress, trauma, guilt, anger, drugs, alcohol and nightmares. I did not know who the enemy was and

39

my ministry was weak and ineffective because of it. Those things that I thought were the enemy, were only signs left along the trail by the real adversary—Satan.

As the weeks and months went by I could plainly see that if I just continued to fight against the "signs," I was going to lose the battle of trying to snatch them from the clutches of their captor. I had been commissioned by God to bring as many as I could to the point of peace that only He can give.

Finally after much prayer, Bible study, and good counsel from some mature brothers, (who knew something about spiritual warfare), I began to get the victory and my ministry took on a whole new meaning. The effectiveness increased when I identified the correct enemy, and applied that knowledge to the lives of my fellow veterans and their families.

Christian soldiers must be wise as serpents (and gentle as doves) in our warfare procedures—we must learn everything God wants us to know about our enemy to be effective on the battlefield.

Let us go to the Holy Scriptures to analyze who we are fighting:

SATAN

The existence of Satan is taught in seven of the Old Testament books and by every New Testament writer. Jesus acknowledged and taught the existence of Satan in Matthew 13:39, and Luke 10:18, 11:18. Satan possesses intellect (2 Cor. 11:3), he has emotions (Rev. 12:17), he has a will (2 Tim. 2:26). Satan is a creature (Ezek. 28:14), he is a spirit being (Eph. 6:11-12), he is a murderer (John 8:44), he is a liar (John 8:44), he is an accuser (Rev. 12:10), and he is the adversary (1 Peter 5:8).

The practice and work of Satan is: He attempts to thwart the work of Christ (Matt. 2:16; John 8:44; Matt. 6:23). He deceives the nations (Rev. 20:3), he blinds the minds of unbelievers (2 Cor. 4:4), he snatches the word from the hearts of unbelievers (Luke 8:12). Satan tempts the Christian (Acts 5:3, 1 Cor. 7:5), he accuses and slanders them (12:10), he hinders the work of Christians (1 Thess. 2:18), he incites persecution against Christians (Rev. 2:10), and he deploys demonic forces against them in an attempt to defeat them (6:11-12).

DEMON FORCES (SATAN'S ARMY)

These are fallen angels. Satan is an angel, and is called prince of the demons (Matt. 12:24). Demons are the well-organized ranks of angels who follow Satan's orders to destroy mankind (Eph. 6:11-12).

The characteristics of demons are: They are unclean spirits, and their doctrine leads to immorality (1 Tim. 4:1-2). They know Jesus (Mark 1:24) and their doom (Matt. 8:29), and the plan of salvation (James 2:19), and they can even be used by God to carrying out His purposes (1 Sam. 16:14; 2 Cor. 12:17).

The warfare tactics of demons are: They attempt to thwart the purpose of God (Dan. 10:10; Rev. 16:13-16). They inflict diseases (Matt. 9:33; Luke 13:11, 16). Demons can possess men (Matt. 4:24), they can possess animals (Mark 5:13). They oppose spiritual growth of God's children (Eph. 6:12), and they disseminate false propaganda, or doctrine (1 Tim. 4:1).

THE PRIMARY BIBLICAL DEFENSES AGAINST SATAN AND HIS ARMY ARE:

A. The believer should use his armor (Eph 6:11-18).

B. Christ intercedes for His followers (John 17:15).

C. The believer has authority to take a stand against Satan (James 4:7).

D. The believer has the authority to invoke the power of the Name of Jesus against any enemy attack and to bind and loose the enemy (Matt. 16:19, John 15:16, Mark 16:17).

WHAT IS SPIRITUAL WARFARE?

It cannot be assumed that every Christian knows what basic spiritual warfare is. Like anything without clear definitions, strange ideas and offbeat practices can evolve.

Spiritual Warfare definition: "Spiritual warfare is using the authority that Christ gave His church to win victories over God's enemies. It surely involves prayer; indeed, prayer is a common form, but it is more than prayer. Prayer may ask God 'Please get the devil away from me.' Warfare uses God's authority to order him away. We fight spiritual warfare in the "heavenly places" (Ephesians 6:12). When the Holy Spirit and His power fill us, we enter this spiritual realm and become discerning of our position and authority there."[1]

As we see in this definition, spiritual warfare isn't always just praying to God; it is doing more. It is using the authority given to us by Jesus to look demons right in the eye and render them ineffective, *"In My name they will cast out demons.* (Mark 16:17b). We do not render evil powers ineffective on our own. Always be mindful that it is God that does the deliverance...not us! We use His authority as His children and heirs; but it is His power, not ours.

By all means, we *must* pray for God to equip and empower us, but we also need to know that He will not necessarily bypass us to clobber the enemy forces. For an example, there are only rare times in Scripture that we find God saying that He will do the fighting *for* us. One is found in Malachi, and interestingly enough, it has to do with our obedience in the area of giving, *"Bring the whole tithe into the storehouse, so that there may be food in My house, and test Me now in this," says the Lord of hosts, "if I will not open for you the windows of heaven, and pour out for you a blessing until it overflows. Then I will rebuke the devourer for you"* (Malachi 3:10–11a). Perhaps more Christians should re-evaluate their views on tithing if they expect to be more victorious in warfare.

Yes, fellow soldier, the Commander expects us to engage the enemy head-on, which isn't strictly praying. We authoritatively command demons to cease their activities and be gone (which is not prayer). It is all done by the power of the blood of Jesus and the authority of His wonderful name. Not a complicated procedure, mind you; just speaking as Jesus would speak.

WARFARE STRATEGIES

The souls of men are the "property" of the strong man (Satan) in Mark 3:27. Satan doesn't have any need for your Mercedes Benz, home, gold, silver, or any other material possession, all he wants to do is take to hell with him as many of us as he can. Christian soldiers need to be snatching the lost from his hands by preaching the gospel at every opportunity and doing spiritual warfare in Jesus' name. We are instructed in that same Scripture (Mark 3:27) to move into action and take that "property"; so we know that it *can* be taken.

It is important to point out here that we seldom, if ever, fight Satan face to face. In all the circumstances that we recognize as "demonic," or "satanic" we must understand that Satan himself is not there directly causing it. He is not omnipresent; he cannot be everywhere there is demonic activity occurring. (That would be like thinking that we are fighting face to face with Ho Chi Minh, when in reality we are engaged in combat with a little Viet Cong who represents Ho.) In fact, Revelation 12:11b tells us where Satan spends most of his time, *"For the accuser of our brethren has been thrown down, who accuses them day and night."* In other words, saints, the devil spends every day and every night before the throne of God accusing us of our sins. How could he himself be in your bedroom causing a quarrel between you and your spouse? It is vital to know that he has sent one of his demonic spirits to cause that quarrel, so address the demon...not Satan!

44

I was at a Point Man veteran meeting one evening back in 1987. As we went around the table making introductions and hearing about how everyone's week had been going, we met one of the demons that Satan sends out to do his work.

One of the veterans complained about an ongoing upheaval in his family. As he began to describe some of the impacting details of his family's problems his countenance began to change. Soon the complaining turned to a full blown demon attack. The vet rose to his feet and gripped the edge of the table in front of him. He began screaming and moaning at the top of his lungs, and we knew that he had to be delivered right away.

We began to assault the enemy with warfare and prayer which went on nonstop for almost two hours. Finally the breakthrough came when the Lord spoke a word of knowledge to one of the brothers. He told him that this man was being controlled by the Vietnamese demon-god, Cau Dai. When we zeroed in and called Cau Dai onto the battlefield by name, he was identified and bound by the name and shed blood of Jesus. We were then able to cast it out of the veteran's life. The man was immediately released from years of agony, and began a brand new walk with Jesus that very hour—even though he had been a professing Christian for over a decade.

The veteran was set free from a specific demon which had tormented him and his family for over thirteen years. He had the victory because we listened to God and called the demon by name just as Jesus did when he called the demon "Legion" to come out of the man in the Book of Mark. When we are doing spiritual warfare, we are fighting against Satan's agents (spirits or fallen angels) dispatched to harass and harm us. We are not fighting him directly! I believe it is fair to say that when we bind and loose, we must bind and loose "the spirit" involved. This gives us much more accuracy in our firepower against the *"...rulers, powers, world forces of this darkness, and spiritual forces of wickedness in the heavenly places"* (Ephesians 6:12).

Important note: You *do not* necessarily need to know the name of every demon you engage in combat. This is a false and deceptive notion from the enemy to weaken your strategy and distract you. In Vietnam, we certainly didn't have to know the name of every Viet Cong soldier before we could shoot at them; and they certainly didn't know our names. We just met on the battlefield and engaged each other in combat. No introductions were necessary—it's the same here. *However, if the Lord does reveal the identity or name of a specific demon, your warfare will be much more effective if you call it by name (see Mark 5:9).*

WEAPONRY

Revelation, chapter 12, offers us an interesting look at some weaponry—both for us and Satan. In order to be the best warriors for the Lord that we can be, we need to know the enemy's strengths...and ours.

It is interesting to note that the weapons on both sides are not of a physical nature, but spiritual, *"For though we walk in the flesh, we do not war according to the flesh, for the weapons of our warfare are not of the flesh, but divinely powerful for the destruction of fortresses"* (2 Corinthians 10:3–4).

Look again at Revelation 12. In verses 9 and 10 we see Satan's weapons—they are in the form of two distinct activities: to *deceive* the world and to *accuse* the brethren. Satan uses these two powerful weapons to run his prison camps and to fight against us—the saints of God. However, the Lord has provided us (the saints) with three defensive weapons to come against the two offensive ones that Satan uses. Ours are described in verse 11: We are to bank on the merits of the death of Christ, *"...they overcame him because of the blood of the Lamb"*; and we are to be active in witnessing, *"...the word of their testimony"*; and we are willing to make any sacrifice for the gospel, including our own death, *"and they did not love their life even to death."*

What wonderful, simple tools God has given us to overcome with. We have His name, *"Whatever you ask of the Father in My name, He may give to you"* (John 15:16). We have the continual cleansing power of His blood, we have the word of our testimony and, (the one that gets Satan the most) we have the carefree hearts to know we are not afraid to sacrifice ourselves (even unto death) for our one and only commander-in-chief...Jesus Christ. These are the most powerful weapons. There are no weapons in all creation that can stand against them.

THE FULL ARMOR
"Put on the full armor of God that you may be able to stand firm against the schemes of the devil" (Ephesians 6:11).

According to the above scripture it is obvious that putting on the armor is crucial in our daily walk (and battles) as a Christian. It is a good practice and discipline to put on God's full armor as we enter into each new day. Many Christians do not take the time or make the effort to pray on their armor before starting out; this usually results in the enemy (Satan) taking advantage of them throughout the day.

When I was in the U.S. Army in Vietnam, we never went on patrol without all our equipment and necessary items to survive combat. Through that experience, I became keenly aware of the importance of being prepared and protected before entering critical situations. Being in God's army is no different, and He expects us to take up His armor daily to repel the assaults of our enemy, and, being a good "Commander," He will never send His troops to the front lines without providing all the equipment they need. Ephesians 6:10–18 and Isaiah 58:8 is that equipment. If we start the day without having the armor on, it is much like being spiritual "streakers"; we may have our earthly clothes on, but we are spiritually naked and vulnerable to the attacks of the devil.

I encourage you to, first of all, study these scriptures (Ephesians 6:10–18, Isaiah 58:8) and then make it a daily discipline to put on the full armor of God in prayer. Here is an example of how to do that (memorization of this procedure is highly suggested):

"I put on the belt of truth, that today I speak and hear only the truth of God.

"I put on the breastplate of righteousness, that my heart is protected by God. That I would have a right standing before God and His throne today.

"I shod my feet with the gospel of peace, that everywhere I step God's peace will abound.

"I take up the shield of faith to ward off the fiery darts of the enemy. Jesus, I proclaim You to be my shield; a shield that I can kneel down behind and seek protection from the enemy.

"I put on the helmet of salvation, that my mind will be protected by God. Lord, transform my mind into the mind of Christ this day, that all thoughts that I have would be the thoughts of Jesus Himself.

"I take up the Sword of the Spirit—the Word of God—to wield against the enemy in time of warfare. I also pray that this Sword may be used to circumcise my own fleshly heart and to give me strength this day to rise above the sin that abounds always in my life and in this world.

"Lord, I thank you for protecting my backside with Your glory as proclaimed in Isaiah 58:8. The Lord God almighty is my rearguard, and I do not have to be afraid of what is behind me. I refuse evil and choose good just as Jesus did. Today, I refuse the will of Satan and choose the will of God!"

WRESTLING

In his spiritual warfare teaching series, Dean Sherman, of Youth With A Mission, mentions a particular fact that is important to spiritual warriors. He calls it "wrestling." He takes the scripture passage of Ephesians 6:12, *"For we wrestle not against flesh and blood..."* and enlightens us further about the nature of our combat. We are in a wrestling match. In this type of match Satan is constantly sending his agents against us to wrestle with us. We cannot say, "Hold it, I'm tired. I need a rest." It is useless to say this because Satan's powers will not back off. If you decide to take a little breather, the demonic enemy will continue to be all over you. They are relentless in their attack. However, one must never get the idea that Satan or his demons have power equal to, or outside, the realm of God's dominion. I have concluded in my years of doing battle that the devil and his demons cannot lay a hand on me unless the Lord lifts His protective hand from me first. He will surely do that if I have unforgiveness and/or practicing sin, or if there is a lesson of growth that God desires in my life (See Job 1:6-12).

Sherman then says, "Like the sport of wrestling, our warfare requires that we be consistent. We have to be alert in our mind (thoughts and imaginations), our heart (attitudes and emotions) and our mouth (spirit power). ...A wrestler wins the wrestling match not only from superior strength, but with knowledge of the holds (wisdom). ...If you walk through life and know the 'wrestling holds,' you can deal with things that come up. ...Walk constantly aware of Satan's schemes—*that's knowing the holds!*" I will add: Make sure that you always have on your full armor (Eph. 6:11). Although we must never take our eyes off Jesus, who is the author and finisher of our faith, I have seen some Christians go overboard, fixing their attention so much on Satan that focusing on God gets "second billing."

" *'We wrestle not against flesh and blood.'* This statement," Sherman goes on to say, "is the key to the whole battle! The key is never battling flesh and blood. The Bible forbids battling flesh and blood. ...You never win by fighting a human being.

"God's kingdom has never been advanced through fighting people. It is advanced only through prayer! When faced with the temptation to fight people, we are to always pray first, resist the devil, assess honestly whether there is any truth in what a person is saying, and then humble ourselves. Don't battle in person (do it in prayer/warfare); continue to agree with God and His Word, keep strong in the faith, and maintain relationships at all costs."

FELLOWSHIP WITH ENEMY FORCES

This is a court-martial offense in any army. A soldier never fraternizes with the enemy. But Christians fellowship with Satan and his hordes without even knowing it. The result is that we give away our footholds—our spiritual "ground."

Holding our ground is of utmost importance to soldiers in war. The ground we have gained by yielding and submitting to God's will is the very thing we need to continually fight for. However, we can lose great portions of our joy and victory (ground) by allowing the enemy access through our thoughts and actions. We can actually forward the enemy's campaign by one thing—SIN!

Every time we sin without repenting (which means turning away and not continuing to do it), we open a window of opportunity for the demons of hell to blow through our lives. The reason Jesus commanded the woman caught in adultery to *"go your way. From now on sin no more"* (John 8:11), was because He knew that her *practice* of sin was what was defeating her.

Every time we practice our sin, we actively fellowship with enemy forces. This action alone gives the devil vital segments of "ground" that has been hard won through our fellowship and obedience to God. (It should be noted that 1 John 1:8 states, *"If we say that we have no sin, we are deceiving ourselves, and the truth is not in us.*") Here is something important to understand: There is a difference in "having" sin and "practicing" sin. Having sin refers to the sin nature which we will have as long as we are on Earth. But practicing sin is the act of continuing to sin over and over with no true repentance. This "practicing" is what Jesus expects all of us to be rid of!

In the best-selling book, *The Bait of Satan,* John Bevere describes the kind of sin most of us practice without even realizing it:

> One of his (Satan's) most deceptive and insidious kinds of bait is something every Christian has encountered—offense. Actually, offense itself is not deadly—if it stays in the trap. But if we pick it up and consume it and feed on it in our hearts, then we have become offended. Offended people produce much fruit, such as hurt, anger, outrage, jealousy, resentment, strife, bitterness, hatred and envy. Some of the consequences of picking up an offense are insults, attacks, wounding, division, separation, broken relationships, betrayal and backsliding.
>
> Often those who are offended do not even realize they are trapped. They are oblivious to their condition because they are so focused on the wrong that was done to them. They are in denial. The most effective way for the enemy to blind us is to cause us to focus on ourselves.[2]

Many Vietnam veterans live with the sin of bitterness and unforgiveness not realizing how destructive it is to them and others.

One summer I was one of the speakers at the national CBN (Christian Broadcasting Network) Vietnam Veterans Conference in Virginia. I was slated to give a workshop on anger management, but God had another plan. He wanted to touch every veteran in attendance in a special way in the area of bitterness and unforgiveness.

Not long after I started talking about anger, the mention of Jane Fonda's blatant betrayal of America during the Vietnam War came up. The following is an account of what I wrote about that session not long after it happened:

> The room was suddenly silent. Every eye was fixed on me as I stood beside the speaker's lectern, and an uneasy feeling gripped me. A nasty little voice on my left shoulder told me that I should run and hide. I stayed, however; not because I was a courageous man, but because God had told me to say what I had just said, and I remained in place only by His strength.
>
> I had just spoken the unspeakable before a group of over two hundred Vietnam veterans, and I was reading every emotion known to man on their faces. Some were shocked with unbelief, many instantly wanted to take me outside, while others looked for reasons to leave the room. The Lord had led me to tell this room full of warriors that I had forgiven Jane Fonda for her misdeeds during the

60's and 70's, and now I was encouraging them to do the same.

After the initial assault on their sense of reality, they allowed me to continue without too much ruckus. Since I was one of them, they figured I deserved to be heard out before they strung me up. I shared with them how God had shown me what harboring unforgiveness for this Vietnam era traitor was doing to my life. He showed me that as long as I couldn't forgive her, I was in relational bondage to her. He spoke this to my heart, "As long as you cannot forgive Jane, you will have a spiritual relationship with her that doesn't please Me."

With this revelation it didn't take me long to repent and forgive this woman. I asked to see a show of hands of those who wanted to be free from this woman and what she represented to them. Needless to say, many hands shot into the air, and as I prayed for deliverance for these men, I heard the crash bars on the exit door bang open. I paused and looked up to see a big Marine in his wheelchair leave the room in a hurry. I later learned that his name was Rob.

Now Rob had been a hard-charging Marine in Vietnam until a machine-gun bullet caught him in the spine. He had been confined to a wheelchair for some twenty years, and been saved only a couple of weeks at the time of the conference. When I saw him leave that day I thought for sure he was going out to his car for a gun. I was relieved to find out that is not why he left the room. He told me later that the last thing he needed to hear was about forgiving Jane Fonda. He may have been a Christian now but there were still a lot of rough edges, so looking back on it I can truly thank the Lord for what developed next.

Thinking that Rob was so disgusted with the idea of forgiving Jane, I sort of shrugged his quick departure off and continued to pray for all the men who had raised their hands.

About an hour after the session we were in the hallway fellowshipping, when we received the surprise of our lives. Rob, who had not been out of his wheel-chair for all those years, walked in the door and marched straight into the cheering arms of the dozens of veterans who had just been set free from their soul bondage of unforgiveness.

I asked Rob what happened, and he said, "I decided to give in and try praying to God that He would let me forgive Jane Fonda. When I said that prayer my legs suddenly began to tingle with feeling. I got so scared that I went straight to the VA hospital and they checked out my legs. Probing around they discovered that I could feel things again. And then I just got up and walked out, leaving my wheelchair behind. Not only am I free from Jane Fonda, but I'm free from my wheelchair too."

This was a glorious moment for all of us. We were allowed a quick peek into the throne room of God while He performed an absolute miracle on this crippled Marine. He showed us that we can all be healed and set free from the traps of the devil if we only obey His Word—if we lay our bitterness upon His altar, and forgive those who have trespassed and offended us in the past.

The best, most powerful spiritual warfare is to cease the practice of sin. Close the window that you opened with your sin by truly repenting. When you do, the enemy has no access to your life.

CHOOSE AND REFUSE

It is important to know that there are some things that Jesus did not inherently bring with Him when He came from heaven to be a man-God. We need to know this because when we fight spiritual warfare we must always know our limitations, what we must submit to, and what actions we are responsible for.

The first of these is mentioned in Isaiah 7:15, *"He knows enough to refuse evil and choose good. For before the boy will know enough to refuse evil and choose good, the land whose two kings you dread will be forsaken."* It is very clear that Immanuel (Jesus) had to learn about refusing and choosing between good and evil. This is an important aspect of our daily warfare. *If he had to learn and practice it, then we should too!* In other words, as we pray each day for God to clothe us in His armor, we must also decide to refuse evil and choose good. It needs to be uttered in prayer and acted upon in life.

The next thing Jesus had to learn was obedience. Hebrews 5:8, *"Although He was a Son, He learned obedience from the things which He suffered."* It would be to our utmost disadvantage to believe that we somehow "naturally" acquire the ability to be obedient. No...we must *learn* it the same as Christ did. He learned it through suffering, and this is why He said that if we are to follow Him we must take up our cross to do it.

In his latest book, *How You Can Shut the Devil's Door,* John Bevere shows us how disobedience to the Lord is the only thing that gives Satan access to our lives. When we learn to walk in complete compliance to His will and word, then we shut down all avenues of attack from the enemy.

It is all a matter of choice. Each day, with our sin-nature lurking, we must make a conscious effort to refuse evil and choose good. We must be willing to suffer and learn obedience. These are tremendously powerful warfare tactics.

Our Authority

Many Christian soldiers are under the belief that individual saints like you and I were never empowered by God to engage demons in combat. I have heard quite a few say things like, "Well, as long as I keep my eyes on Jesus I never have to confront demons. He will confront them for me." This is a nice thought, but not too scriptural. Keeping our eyes on Jesus is definitely scriptural, but so are His orders for us to use His authority to face demons in combat!

I have also heard some brothers and sisters mention that Jesus only gave authority to the twelve disciples to cast out demons and conduct spiritual warfare on His behalf. This is

THE ACT OF WAR

not true. He has given all of us the authority to do spiritual warfare in His name, all the time!

Let's look at the Word of God to see evidence of our authority in doing spiritual warfare:

Luke 10:17 says, *"And the seventy returned with joy, saying, 'Lord, even the demons are subject to us in Your Name.'"*

Jesus had commissioned seventy other believers (just ordinary ones like you and I) at the beginning of Luke 10 to go out ahead of Him and prepare the people for ministry. He sent them in pairs. In verse 17 they returned to Him and gave a report. He (Jesus) then affirms them in verse 19, *"Behold, I have given you authority to tread upon serpents and scorpions, and over all the power of the enemy, and nothing shall injure you."*

So you see, we all, to this day, have that God-given authority to do face-to-face warfare with satanic forces. To say anything different is anti-Christ and whispered rumors from the enemy's camp. Assume your authority from the Word of God and nowhere else.

BALANCE

Balance should be one of the most sought after positions in the Christian life. To be out of balance is an open door to weird practices, and even cultic beliefs and activities. In spiritual warfare, we must have balance or our good efforts can be subverted, and even end up in the enemy hands.

In the same chapter in Luke (Chapter 10:20), we see Jesus commanding His followers to a life of balance, *"Nevertheless do not rejoice in this, that the spirits are subject to you, but rejoice that your names are recorded in heaven."* What He is saying is that now that we have this authority and are equipped to overcome the enemy in His name, we are not to become embroiled in the activity of warfare to the degree that we lose the joy of our salvation...nothing is more important to focus on than the sheer fact that we are going to heaven. Hallelujah!

Have you ever heard of someone having a "deliverance ministry"? In other words, they specialize in exorcism. Nowhere in the Word of God is there a mention of such a specialized thing. Sure, we are given authority to cast out demons, and have power over the enemy; but every ministry is a deliverance ministry, and every minister (or lay person, as far as that goes) is a deliverance minister. That's just plain old Bible practice! No one has a corner on delivering people from the hands of Satan. We all have the same authority and commission to do it. That's balance.

WEARING-OUT TACTICS OF SATAN

When Satan launches an attack, don't expect it to always be noticeable at first. He is a master of guerrilla tactics; almost always done by clandestine methods, and never with a pattern. One of the methods of attack is the subtle "wearing-out" tactic that Watchman Nee writes about in his book *Let Us Pray:*

"And he shall speak words against the Most High, and shall wear out the saints of the Most High" (Daniel 7:25).

Satan has a work which is wearing out the children of God. His attack may not come suddenly; oftentimes, it comes gradually and slowly. Daniel 7:25 mentions how Satan shall wear out the saints of the Most High. In fact, Satan has a plan against the saints of the Most High, which is to wear them out. Hence let us clearly recognize thatthe work of Satan in the lives of God's children is frequently not very noticeable, since his work is slowly to wear them down.

What is the meaning of the phrase, "wear out"? It has in it the idea of reducing a little this minute, then reducing a little further the next minute. Reduce a little today and reduce a little tomorrow. Thus the wearing is almost imperceptible; nevertheless, it is a reducing. The wearing down is scarcely an activity of which is conscious, yet the end result is that there is nothing left.[3]

Wearing out the physical body:

Especially with respect to the human body, we may easily see how the enemy wears out the children of God...(sickness and poor health).... We ought to point out how many of the Lord's servants, before they went forth to preach the gospel, were in good health, but that after they went out to work for the Lord their health failed in a short period of three to five years. This is the enemy wearing out the saints...[4]

Wearing out man's heart:

Not only does he work on the body, Satan also works in the human heart. Upon first believing in the Lord you may feel very happy, joyful and peaceful. But if you are not watchful—being ignorant of what the enemy can do— you will find yourself one day mysteriously uncomfortable.... Little by little, your peace is completely lost, your joy totally gone. This is the way the devil wears you down to a state of fatigue and despair.[5]

Wearing out our spiritual life:

He will take away our prayer life little by little, and cause you to trust God less and less and yourself more and more, a little at a time.... What is so wickedly subtle about Satan, though, is that he does not strike with one grand stroke; instead, he will employ the tactic of wearing out the saints over an extended period of time, thus causing God's children to lose out and backslide a little at a time...(it's gradualism).[6]

Gradualism is exemplified by the "How to boil a frog" story. To cook a live frog you don't throw it into scalding hot water, because he will just jump out due to the heat. Instead, you throw him in cool water and let it gradually come up to boiling and the frog never knows it's being cooked until it's too late.

Wearing out our time:

Felix often sent for Paul and communed with him. After two years of conversation with the powerful and gifted apostle, he was still unsaved."[7]

Imagine how many others could have been saved by Paul if he had not spent all that time on one person who was determined not to know Jesus as his savior. There are times when a person with a need comes and you begin to help them. And then one thing leads to another, and before you know it you are baby-sitting them; and they believe they cannot live without you. They cannot see Jesus...and actually refuse to see Him; because as long as they have you to take care of them, then they don't need Jesus. It is subtle, but it happens all the time. This is a "wearing-out" tactic of the devil.

In conclusion, we ought to read Ephesians 6:13, in which Paul writes that we, 'having done all' ought 'to stand'; we must stand, and not allow Satan to continue wearing us down. We should ask the Lord to open our eyes to see what wearing-out work Satan is performing on the children of God. May we rise up to resist and to speak against the enemy. May we declare: 'I resist, I oppose, I do not accept such wearing down.'

Such a word needs the covering of the blood. May God cover us with the blood.[8]

Let me conclude this chapter with this: Every person who does not know Jesus as Lord and Savior is a P.O.W. (prisoner of war). We need to launch raids behind enemy lines to set them free...one by one...regardless of where they are found. This is the largest "hostage incident" in the history of mankind, and as Christian soldiers we need to begin viewing the unsaved world as just that. We must rescue our fellow humans from the hands of the enemy oppressors, and we can only do that by leading them to our Lord and Savior, Jesus Christ.

CHAPTER FOUR

ENEMY TACTICS

TRIPWIRES, BOOBY TRAPS, AND AMBUSHES

I was part of the first American forces that shipped off to Southeast Asia to fight the Vietnam War in 1965. As individuals in these fighting units, we not only served our country with our lives, but we also blindly entangled ourselves with unseen forces of the spirit realm. Many of us bonded with the Asian people and were exposed to the heavy demonic practices which are prevalent in that area of the world. Some veterans are still plagued today by the satanic curses and harassment of the enemy. In fact, the debilitating effects of Post-Traumatic Stress (PTS)—which I wrote in detail about in *Nam Vet: Making Peace with Your Past* (Multnomah Press, 1990),— certainly has it's root of power through many of these evil practices that we participated in *and condoned* while in Asia.

After becoming a believer in Christ, I spent many years working with Vietnam veterans. Not long after I started in this ministry, I began to re-evaluate the purpose and thrust of reaching these men for Jesus. This happened when I went through a particularly dramatic deliverance/warfare session one evening in the back room of a local church. The veteran who got delievered had been a solid Christian for thirteen years. After he was set free from a powerful Asian demon, I knew God was showing us how the Vietnam War was still raging in supernatural ways, and He wanted us to begin a new level of warfare.

I began to search the Word of God for answers and quickly saw how much God has intended for us to be. Not just saved saints, but equipped soldiers who go to war daily against the schemes of the devil. Then, after reading Wilbur Pickering's "Chapter VI," (Chapter Two of this book), I became convinced that most of the lingering problems of Vietnam vets have a spiritual base to them. I knew that if veterans were not getting healed and set free from the symptoms of PTS by turning to God, then there was demonic bondage that needed to be dealt with. The army of God needs to know more about how the enemy conducts his war against human beings. The Vietnam War provides us with a good proving ground on the topic.

To understand what really happened to our troops in Southeast Asia, and why they are seemingly "incurable cases" (according to the secular view of the Veteran's Administration and vet centers across the country), we must look from the spiritual side of things. The secular professionals do not consider these problems to have a spiritual basis, but as Christians we must primarily view the eternal, not the physical, in such life-changing matters.

Before the United States got involved in Vietnam, France had been occupying the country for many years. France failed to keep peace between the warring tribes and were ousted because of it. History reveals that in the areas of Vietnam, Laos, Cambodia and Thailand there have been century-old battles between these tribes.

During that time, much of the religion in these areas was Buddhist and Hindu, mixed with Spiritism (worshipping spirits). Over the centuries, this part of the world was given over to pagan spiritual powers (see Ephesians 6:10–12). When they went to war they called upon their gods—rulers and powers—and spirits to fight for them and guide them in combat. In the midst of these bloody battles, they learned how to call on the spirits to destroy their opposition. When foreign powers came to their countries, they used these same spiritual forces against them as well. Now, here is the crux of what happened to our American troops—they were prepared to fight a physical war and had no idea that a spiritual one was even being fought! They were spiritually ambushed and tricked. Much sickness, pain and death has followed our veterans since.

ALLOWING THE ENEMY ENTRANCE

In an effort to make peace and be friendly with the people of Southeast Asia, whom they were sent to fight for and protect, many young Americans participated in rituals and cus-

toms of foreign gods. Consequently, they fell under the influence of these evil powers and had no way to fight them. Our
young, exuberant soldiers had no idea what they were invit-
ing into their lives, and the curses and demonic possession
swept them away.

A picture-perfect example of this "friendship" with the
devil amongst Americans in Vietnam is vividly seen in the
January 1965 edition of <u>National Geographic</u>. It gives witness—to include blood sacrifices—to a U.S. Army Special
Forces captain [Gillespie] participating in rituals, ceremonies
and even combat, involving powers of darkness. Gillespie was
an advisor to the Rhade tribe fighting against communist
forces. Here is an excerpt from that article: *"...He* [Yjohn] *and
Gillespie—who were already blood brothers in the Rhade tribe—
would undergo a ceremony of alliance with Captain Truong and
invoke the protection of the spirits. Gillespie agreed and Yjhon
hurried away to alert his sorcerer..."*

It does not take a rocket scientist to figure out that this
American Green Beret was "dancing with the devil" in order
to accomplish his mission. Our men and women were placed
right in the line of fire of much demonic activity, and most
were casualties who still suffer today from the effects of it.

I recently read an article from Generals of Intercession,
Cindy Jacob's ministry, about their recent trip to Viet Nam.
The newsletter, <u>G.I. News</u>, reminded me of the incredible
spiritual battle that veterans of Vietnam are still in. While
serving in Point Man Ministries, I heard that Buddhist monks
had prayed curses upon the Americans that came to Viet-

nam. The article re-enforced my beliefs in this clandestine effort to disrupt the lives of so many young Americans. The three specific curses reportedly cast upon our servicemen were:

1) That they would be wandering men the rest of their lives.
2) That they would never find peace.
3) That they would be angry forever.

Since we know that Satan's playground and battlefield is mostly in the minds of men, we began to take notice of how these alleged curses have affected so many Vietnam veterans. When we took serious stock in this hidden tactic of the enemy, the origin of PTS took on a new meaning.

FIRST AID

Curses are absolutely real, and the Holy Bible is full of descriptive examples. All one has to do is look at the shattered and confused lives of many, many Vietnam vets to see the fruit of them. Those three curses—wandering, no peace and angry—is the exact duplicate of many troubled lives of veterans in America today. I believe these curses are still causing havoc in many lives, even the lives of Christian believers!

So what are curses? A curse is defined as: "uttering a wish of evil against one; to imprecate evil; to call for mischief or injury to fall upon; to execrate, to bring evil upon or to blast, vex, harass or torment with great calamities" (Merriam Webster's Collegiate Dictionary).

Curses are activated through the spoken word. The Scriptures tell us that words are not mere sounds on the lips, but life and death are in the power of the tongue. Words are agents sent forth for good or bad—for ourselves or for others. (Read about the blessings and cursings in Deuteronomy 27–30, and when Jesus cursed the fig tree in Mark 11).

When people cannot get free, there is *always* a reason. Sometimes it is due to disobedience and lack of submission to God (because of curses that haven't been broken by invoking the power of the name and shed blood of Jesus Christ of Nazareth). Curses act as shields and fences around demon spirits. These evil spirits can be invoked to manifest during ministry, but they will not and cannot come out until the curses have been discovered (discerned) and then broken.

During my years of ministry with Point Man, I saw hundreds of veterans break free from those curses by taking these two steps:

Step One: Read Galatians 3:13 and Colossians 2:14 aloud.

Step Two: Pray the following prayer aloud:

Heavenly Father, in the name of Jesus Christ, I am truly Your child. I have been purchased by the shed blood of Jesus. I belong to You. I do not belong to the devil. The devil has no right to me and no power over me as long as I am obedient to Your will and because of the precious blood of Jesus. Father, You have known my sins. I confess them all. I repent of them all now. I ask You to forgive me. Forgive me of every sin and remove the stains out of my heart and my life—for Your Word tells me that when I confess my sin, You will be faithful to forgive me and will cleanse me of all unrighteousness. I not only confess my own sin, but I confess the sins that were committed by my parents, grandparents and great-grandparents—sins which introduced curses into my family line. I confess those sins to You that the power of the curse might be broken through the shed blood of the Lord Jesus Christ.

In the name of Jesus, I now rebuke, break, and loose myself and my family from my own sins, the sins of my ancestors or from any other person. I am redeemed from the curse of the law. With the authority placed in me by my redeemed position in Jesus, I break the power of every evil word that has knowingly or unknowingly been spoken against me by any other person, cult or spirit. I cancel that spoken word and the power of that curse in the authority of the name of Jesus Christ.

I command every spirit which has come in the door of that curse to leave me now...in the name of Jesus Christ.

The Parallels of War

My wife and I have been asked to speak at many veteran's events over the years. Once, when we were preparing our ministry materials, an interesting discussion arose about enemy warfare tactics. For one of my wife's workshop sessions she needed to know about some of the ways the communist forces fought against us in Vietnam. Not being a veteran, she was busy picking my brain. As we talked, both of us realized that many of the ways the Viet Cong fought their guerrilla-style warfare was much the same as how Satan fights us. We found the parallels to be so enlightening that they are worth mentioning in this manual.

As I wrote about with great detail in *Nam Vet: Making Peace with Your Past*, the differences in how both sides fought the war in Vietnam were somewhat extreme. The communists primarily used guerilla warfare because they were outgunned and were technologically disadvantaged to fight us. Therefore, they chose to use hit-and-run tactics and small unit actions to wear us down, and to catch us off guard. They avoided direct contact (conventional) combat as much as possible.

The following list of ways the enemy fought is by no means complete, but it will serve to show you some of the tactics used by the Viet Cong (VC) and North Vietnamese soldiers to kill, maim, harrass and disrupt our war strategies. You will see how these methods match Satan's ways in fighting us in the spirit realm.

1) The VC attempted to look as much like the civilian population as possible. (Satan disguises himself and can even look like a friend—an angel of light.)

2) The VC did not fight for physical territory...they fought to win the hearts and minds of people. (If Satan can shift our attention, our zeal, our time, our hearts and our minds onto something other than Jesus and the Great Commission, he has won. We have fallen into idolatry without even knowing it. He has captured our heart and mind, leaving us unfruitful and ineffective in the Kingdom of God.)

3) The VC deployed boobytraps along trails to destroy our confidence. By blowing off the arms and legs of our

buddies along the march, our purpose and confidence was weakened. We were taking casualties, but never saw the enemy because after the explosives were detonated the enemy could watch the destruction from afar—out of harm's way. (Satan knows he cannot win the war, but if he can set enough traps along our walk to make us hurt and be unsure of our faith then he can keep us from being effective witnesses for Christ. He usually wreaks enough misery from a distance that we sometimes forget who the real foe is. Many times we target each other as the enemy because he (the devil) is not an obvious player in the scenario).

4) The VC used innocent civilians, even to the point of destroying them, as decoys to undermine our security and confidence. It was a common practice to strap explosive charges on small children and send them into groups of G.I.s to make friends and win their affection. When the child would get close enough, the communist soldier would detonate the charge with a remote switch—taking out the G.I.s and the child. (Often Satan will use even good things to win our affections. Once he has accomplished this, he ambushes us and attempts to destroy us).

5) The VC tried to get us to mistakenly kill our fellow warriors. One particular tactic he used was what we called "cutting the pie." At night, when we would stop daylight operations in the jungle, we would dig into night-defensive positions. The entire unit formed into a large circle

(pie) for protection. Normally there were two men to a hole, and one slept while the other kept watch for enemy activity. The VC would probe a point in the perimeter circle, making a lot of noise to attract attention, and would try to take a slice out of the "pie." After making the noise, they would pull back into the jungle and hope we would fire our weapons in the direction of the noise—which would be at our own men on the other side of the circle. (Satan deploys the same strategy against us. He creeps into our midst and causes disruptive "noise," and then pulls back into his jungle and waits for us to kill each other. He tries his best to cause fights, quarrels, dissatisfaction and dissension in our midst. All the while he has distanced himself and remains the undetected source of trouble. This tactic is evident in almost every church or fellowship in Christendom. Most pastors can attest to this.)

6) The VC attempted to stay close to U.S. military units. They knew that the closer they could be to us—especially in a firefight—the less likely it was that we would call in artillery or air support, in fear of directing the incoming fire on ourselves. (Satan sends his forces against us in the same manner. He gets as close to us as possible so that we cannot determine which direction to call in "air support" to take him out. Many times he is so close that we completely overlook him when he is in our midst.)

As I mentioned before, this is only a small portion of the hundreds of ways the enemy can come against us. I hope it helps you become more alert in the future.

THE SOLDIER'S CHALLENGE

As one of Satan's P.O.W.s, you were once bound up in an out-of-the-way cage somewhere. You could not fight because of fear and bondage. Satan centered his attacks on those soldiers who escaped from his prison by the power of the Holy Spirit—they are his only threat. Since Christ's chosen soldiers are determined to set free all the captives Satan has in bondage, you pose a huge problem for him.

Yes, we are at war. It is a covert war, but a war none the less. Covert means that it is undercover, out of sight and out of mind. For the most part, it is an unseen war. When a slave soldier from Satan's army is liberated and joins God's, he becomes like a beacon in a stormy, dark night. Satan is afraid the other captive soldiers may see His light in us and likewise be attracted to it. He sees the threat and lives in fear that he will lose more soldiers to God by them seeing your bright light. He will slander you; he will make you look unworthy because of the terrible things you have done in your past; and he will try to get you to turn back to your old ways so he can blackmail you. When all these things happen, your light can begin to draw dim. You may not feel worthy enough to even be called a Christian. Sin does that—it makes us wary of witnessing and proclaiming the name of Jesus. This is psychological warfare at its best.

I challenge you to get into the fight, be filled with the Holy Spirit, and go about the business of setting the captives free! Is it going to be easy? Is it going to be comfortable? No, it isn't. Is it going to be rewarding? Absolutely! Let us be soldiers of the cross as Jesus would have us be.

"You therefore must endure hardship as a good soldier of Jesus Christ. No one engaged in warfare entangles himself with the affairs of this life, that he may please him who enlisted him as a soldier" (2 Timothy 2:4).

THE ARMY IN WHICH I CHOOSE TO FIGHT

"For day by day men came to David to help him, until there was a great army like the army of God" (1 Chronicles 12:22).

God's people have two armies. One set up for display with lovely guns, neat little soldiers—all-in-a-row, socially-correct staffs schooled in etiquette—and distinguished generals swaggering through the ranks as if they were something in themselves. It's core is made of sunshine soldiers and fair-weather patriots who leave the dirty work to others. This army shows itself for a modest fee on any Sunday morning parade ground, one steeped in traditional salutes, precision drills, and weekend-warrior stamina.

The other is a real army, composed entirely of enthusiastic soldier/saints in battle attire, who will not be put on display, but from whom impossible efforts are demanded. Their standard is the Word of God. The Sword of Truth is their primary weapon. This is the army in which I choose to fight.

Occasionally I meet other soldiers who've made this choice. When I do, it's like an old soldier's dream; where the team is a team—everyone respecting the other's spiritual gifts and God-given authority, as if observing an unwritten law unto ourselves. And leading by humble experience, the generals, colonels, lieutenants and sergeants all follow the tough commandments of God's written Word. There is no compromise. This is the army in which I choose to fight.

Chuck Dean

ENDNOTES

[1] Gehlhar, Philip. *Power for Warfare, Discerning and Defeating God's Enemies*, (Mukilteo, WA: WinePress, 1995), page 1-3.

[2] Bevere, John. *The Bait of Satan, Your Response Determines Your Future*, (Orlando, FL: Creation House, 1994), page 10.

[3] Nee, Watchman. *Let Us Pray*, (New York, NY: Christian Fellowship Publishers, Inc., 1977), pages 79-87.

[4] Ibid

[5] Ibid

[6] Ibid

[7] Ibid

[8] Ibid

Read these other great veteran titles!

Point Man in Your Pocket - 40 Day Devotional
By Chuck Dean
WinePress Publishing, 68 pages, softcover $2.99

In God We Trust - New Testament for Veterans & Active Duty
Introduction by Chuck Dean, translation by Gleason Ledyard
WinePress Publishing, 564 pages, softcover (camouflage) $7.99

Nam Vet, Making Peace with Your Past
By Chuck Dean
Multnomah Books, 154 pages, softcover $9.99

Mortal Midnight
By Danny Daniels
WinePress Publishing, 230 pages, softcover $11.99

Secret Weapon: Men Overcoming Chaos
By Lt.Col. (ret) Dave Winecoff with Chuck Dean
WinePress Publishing, 208 pages, softcover $9.99

The Broken Sword
By Lee Westbrook
Nissi Publishing, 260 pages, softcover $12.95

The Jesus Nut
By David B. Freeman
Nissi Publishing, 308 pages, softcover $12.95

Scars of War
By Paul Tribus
Companion Press, 98 pages, softcover $6.95

How to Overcome Anger, Bitterness & Unforgiveness
By Paul Tribus
WinePress Publishing, 112 pages, softcover $8.95

Running on Empty
By Stan Gorman
Vinberg & Associates, 140 pages, softcover $9.95

Order by calling the WinePress Order Line toll-free at
800-917-BOOK

To order additional copies of *Behind Enemy Lines*
send $6.99 + $2.95 shipping and handling to:

WinePress Publishing
PO Box 1406
Mukilteo, WA 98275

•

Have your credit card ready and call:

(800) 917-BOOK

•

Or order through our online bookstore at
http://www.winepresspub.com

FOR VETERAN RELATED ISSUES AND MINISTRY
OPPORTUNITIES, CONTACT:

Point Man International Ministries
PO Box 339
Sheridan, MI 48884-0339
(517) 831-5215
(517) 831-5216 - (Fax)
(800) 877-VETS - (Hotline)
http://www.mcpages.com/PointMan/ - (Home Page)